Contents

Meet our neighbours

Geography is the what of where. It is vitally important for understanding the world around us. Geographers question the world and seek to understand it, they explain why things are where they are.

Francesca Carter – Geographer

Australia has interesting neighbours. To Australia's east, New Zealand has a wealth of mountains and hot springs. North of New Zealand, island nations such as Vanuatu and Fiji dot the oceans. To Australia's north, Papua New Guinea, Timor-Leste and Indonesia are rich with forests, jungles and mountains. These nations are all home to people with interesting cultures and stories.

Australians live in a wonderful neighbourhood!

Did you know?
Many of Australia's neighbours have active volcanoes on land and under nearby seas. Auckland, the largest city of New Zealand, is built on the site of about 50 **dormant** volcanoes.

dormant sleeping; not active

Beautiful carvings are popular in Bali, Indonesia.

LET'S FIND OUT

- Which nations are near Australia?
- How are these countries similar to and different from each other?
- What geographical features make these countries special?
- How are these countries different from Australia?
- What can we learn about their people?

Briony's boating blog

Briony and her dad are on a sailing trip. They are visiting some of Australia's neighbours. Briony is writing a blog about the trip for her class.

Day 1 – New Zealand

We started our trip in Milford Sound. It is in the South Island of New Zealand. New Zealand has two main islands.

Milford Sound is a **fjord**.

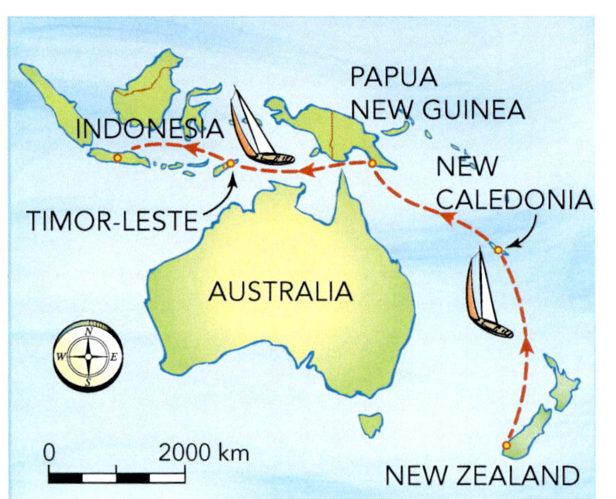

A map of our trip

Day 10 – New Caledonia

Today we arrived at New Caledonia. It is a group of pretty islands. Its main island is called Grande Terre. A mountain **range** runs along its middle.

Along the east side, trees and plants grow thickly. On the other side, the land is drier and more open.

Grande Terre

fjord a long area of water with steep cliffs on both sides
range a line of mountains joined together

Day 15 –
Papua New Guinea

Our next stop is Port Moresby. This is a city in Papua New Guinea. This is a country of rainforests. Mountains run through its middle.

Port Moresby

Day 20 – Timor-Leste

Today we reached Timor-Leste (East Timor). Timor-Leste is on the east end of the island of Timor. It has many forests and mountains. It is warm and damp here.

Day 24 – Indonesia

Today we reached Java. It is one of Indonesia's many islands. It has mountains from east to west. They were formed by volcanoes. It also has large rainforests. Lots of people live here.

Wild animals live in rainforests in Java.

_ _ _ _ _ _ _ _ _ _

damp wet

Breakaway tasks

Remembering

1 In which island of New Zealand is Milford Sound?

2 How were the mountains of Java formed?

Understanding

3 Draw the natural features in the blog, for example, 'mountains'.

4 Write a quiz about two countries that Briony visited. Swap quizzes with a partner.

Applying

5 On a map, find another place Briony could have visited. Trace or copy the map of their journey and add this place.

6 Make a timeline of Briony and her dad's journey.

Analysing

7 Discuss with a partner why Briony and her dad visited the places in the order they did.

Evaluating

8 Which place on Briony's journey would you most like to visit? Write three reasons.

9 Look at a map. What other places could Briony and her dad visit? Choose one place. Research and write facts about one geographical feature of this place.

Creating

10 Research one of the places mentioned. Prepare a talk for the class on this place. Include images.

Visit vibrant Vanuatu!

Are you looking for an exciting holiday?
Come to vibrant Vanuatu!

Vanuatu is full of beautiful places. It has rainforests, mountains, volcanoes and waterfalls. It's also the best place for adventure.

Try climbing the roots of the banyan tree ...

Vanuatu is made up of 82 lovely islands. They stretch for 1330 kilometres. The largest is called Espiritu Santo. Vanuatu's highest mountain, Mount Tabwemasana, is found here. It's 1879 metres tall and it's the perfect place for trekking and climbing. Vanuatu is home to giant banyan trees – some of the world's biggest trees.

Beautiful Efate Island

vibrant full of life and energy

Vanuatu has many volcanoes. Its most famous is Mount Yasur, on the island of Tanna. Its **crater** is 400 metres wide. It has been erupting for 800 years, but is usually safe to visit.

Guides take tourists up Mount Yasur.

Vanuatu is great for outdoor activities. These include fishing, kayaking and mountain biking. It has warm weather, too. November to April is hot and wet. The rest of the year is cooler and drier.

Visit Vanuatu for a feast of tropical treasures!

crater a bowl-shaped area at the top of a volcano

Breakaway tasks

Remembering

1 How many islands make up Vanuatu?

2 What kind of mountain is Mount Yasur?

Understanding

3 Summarise the information about Vanuatu in your own words.

Applying

4 Research to find out more about Vanuatu. Write to a friend about a place you could enjoy visiting.

5 Trace a map of Vanuatu. Label the places mentioned. Which countries are its neighbours?

Analysing

6 Find and write out the words the author has used to excite you about visiting Vanuatu.

7 List four questions about daily life that you would ask someone who lives in Vanuatu.

Evaluating

8 Does the brochure make you want to visit Vanuatu? What other information would help you make up your mind about having a holiday there?

9 How different is Vanuatu from where you live? Make a Similar and different chart.

Creating

10 Make a fact file about Vanuatu. Present it on paper in the shape of a feature of Vanuatu, e.g. a volcano or mountain.

Make a koru necklace

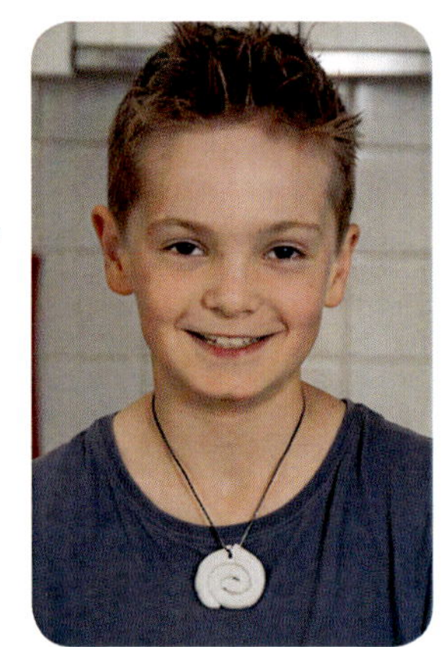

Maori people have made bone carvings for many years. A popular carving is a fern leaf as it opens up. This shape is called a koru. It stands for growth and peace.

Here's how to make your own koru necklace.

You will need
- string
- air-drying clay
- a chopstick

Steps

1 Roll some clay into a sausage shape. Make the two ends round.

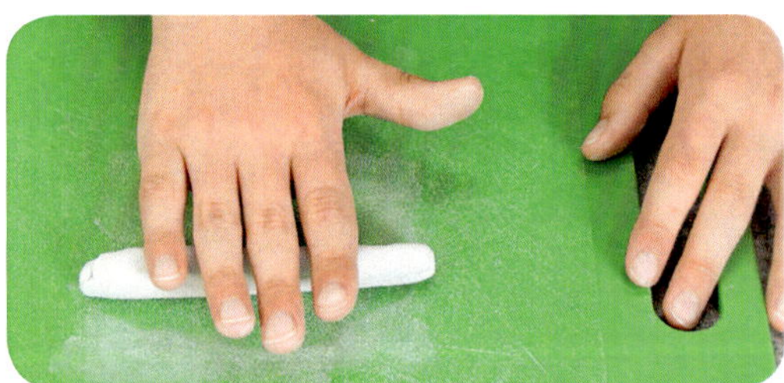

2 Bend the clay into a curved shape, like a snail.

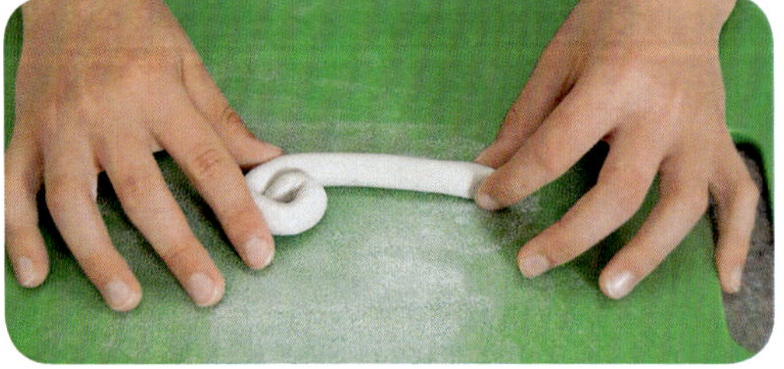

3 Use a chopstick. Make a small hole in the top of the shape.

4 Let the clay dry and harden for 24 hours.

5 Thread the string through the hole. Tie the ends together. Your koru is ready to wear!

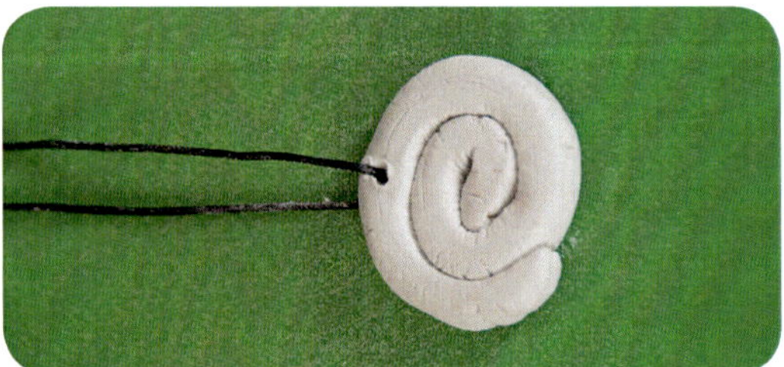

Maori the first people to live in New Zealand

Breakaway tasks

Remembering

1 Where are the Maori people from?

2 What does the koru stand for?

Understanding

3 Answer True or False to each statement.

a Maori people have made bone carvings.

b The clay should be rolled into a ball shape.

c The clay dries in about 24 hours.

4 Research and draw a real koru leaf.

Applying

5 Demonstrate this procedure to someone who hasn't seen the text.

6 Copy or trace a map of New Zealand. Label three key features.

Analysing

7 Think of shapes from nature that would work as a necklace. Draw and label them.

Evaluating

8 Research jewellery made by Aboriginal or Torres Strait Islander people. Which is your favourite? Why?

9 List and draw two other shapes in nature that could stand for growth and peace.

Creating

10 Design your own jewellery, based on another natural shape. Make it and explain it to the class.

The crocodile story

A legend is a story that is passed down from one generation to the next. It has important meaning for the culture it comes from. This story is from Timor-Leste (East Timor).

Many years ago a small crocodile lived in a swamp in a far away place. He dreamed of becoming a big crocodile but as food was **scarce**, he became weak and grew sadder and sadder.

He left for the open sea, to find food and **realise** his dream, but the day became increasingly hot and he was still far from the seashore. The little crocodile was rapidly drying out and lay down to die.

generation group of people of similar age
scarce hard to find
realise make something happen

A small boy took pity on the **stranded** crocodile and carried him to the sea.

The crocodile, instantly **revived**, was grateful. "Little boy," he said, "you have saved my life. If I can ever help you in any way, please call me. I will be at your command ..."

A few years later, the boy called the crocodile, who was now big and strong. "Brother Crocodile," he said, "I too have a dream. I want to see the world."

"Climb on my back," said the crocodile, "and tell me, which way do you want to go?"

"Follow the Sun," said the boy.

stranded stuck somewhere
revived feeling better

The crocodile set off for the east, and they travelled the oceans for years, until one day the crocodile said to the boy, "Brother, we have been travelling for a long time. But now the time has come for me to die. In memory of your kindness, I will turn myself into a beautiful island, where you and your children can live until the Sun sinks in the sea."

As the crocodile died, he grew and grew, and his **ridged** back became the mountains and his scales the hills of Timor.

Now when the people of East Timor swim in the ocean, they enter the water saying, "Don't eat me, crocodile, I am your **relative**."

ridged long and raised
relative a family member

Breakaway tasks

Remembering

1 Where did the crocodile first live?

2 What became of the crocodile's scales when he died?

Understanding

3 Make up three quiz questions about the story. Ask them to a partner.

4 Find pictures of Timor-Leste (East Timor) that show what the story is about.

Applying

5 Locate Timor-Leste on a map. Write down the capital city. What are its neighbours? How far is it from Australia?

6 Write a sequence of the events in the story in your own words.

Analysing

7 What do you think is the most important event in the story? What might have happened if this event did not happen? Discuss your ideas with a partner.

Evaluating

8 Write what is your favourite part of the story. Why?

9 What is the message of this legend? Write in your own words.

Creating

10 Create a comic strip or cartoon based on this legend.

Strands in action

Core tasks

1. Choose a country near Australia (not Vanuatu) that interests you. Research what makes it special.
   - Design a brochure to bring visitors to this country.
2. List the geographical features in Australia (e.g. mountains, rivers, deserts).
   - Choose one of Australia's neighbours.
   - Research features that are the same and different.
   - Present your information to the class in an interesting way.

Extra tasks

1. Make a word find puzzle using the names of Australia's neighbours. Include city names and country names.
2. Research music that is part of the culture of one of Australia's neighbours, for example, Maori songs. Find a song and share it with the class.
3. Design a coat of arms for a country you have learnt about. Use the country's geographical features, plants or animals on it.
4. On a map, find an island to the west of Australia (e.g. Christmas Island). Make a fact file. Include how far this island is from Australia, how many people live there and how big the island is.

When writing a procedure, break the process into short, easy steps. Write one simple instruction for each step. This makes it easier for readers to follow it.